Assyrian Mythology

Gods and Religion of Ancient Mesopotamia

© **Copyright 2023 – Creek Ridge Publishing All rights reserved.**

The content contained within this book may not be reproduced, duplicated or transmitted without direct written permission from the author or the publisher.

Under no circumstances will any blame or legal responsibility be held against the publisher, or author, for any damages, reparation, or monetary loss due to the information contained within this book, either directly or indirectly.

Legal Notice:

This book is copyright protected. It is only for personal use. You cannot amend, distribute, sell, use, quote or paraphrase any part, or the content within this book, without the consent of the author or publisher.

Disclaimer Notice:

Please note the information contained within this document is for educational and entertainment purposes only. All effort has been executed to present accurate, up to date, reliable, complete information. No warranties of any kind are declared or implied. Readers acknowledge that the author is not engaging in the rendering of legal, financial, medical or professional advice. The content within this book has been derived from various sources. Please consult a licensed professional before attempting any techniques outlined in this book.

By reading this document, the reader agrees that under no circumstances is the author responsible for any losses, direct or indirect, that are incurred as a result of the use of information contained within this document, including, but not limited to, errors, omissions, or inaccuracies.

Table of Contents

Introduction 1

Chapter 1: Basics of Assyrian Mythology 5

    The Beliefs of Assyria Mythology 5
    Temples and Shrines 9
    The Afterlife 11
    Omens and Signs 12
    The Types Gods of Assyria 13

Chapter 2: Gods 18

    Ashur 18
    Anu 20
    Enlil 23
    Enki 26
    Connecting with the Deities 28

Chapter 3: Goddesses 31

    Inanna 31
    Ninhursag 36

    Ereshkigal 39
    Connecting with the Deities 42

Chapter 4: Demigods and Heroes 43
    Adapa 44
    Enkidu 46
    Lugalbanda 48
    Shamhat 49
    Sammu-rammat 51

Chapter 5: Practices 55
    Main practices in Assyrian Mythology 56
    Childbirth 59
    Private Devotions 62

Conclusion 64

References 66

Introduction

Like many other belief systems hailing from this region, Assyrian mythology had an incredibly long-standing effect on other cultures and religions. Flourishing between 1900 BCE to 650 CE, Assyria has unique historical significance in the scheme of Mesopotamian mythology. Some of the most indicative archeological evidence of the beliefs of Mesopotamian mythology comes from the ancient Assyrian territories. From the tablets and other forms of writing and art found in this region, scholars have established that Assyrian beliefs were laced with tales about powerful gods, goddesses, demigods, heroes, and mythical beings whose actions helped explain events that contradicted mundane reasoning and ideas.

Given that the origins of Assyrian mythology can be traced back to the Near East, it's not surprising that the beliefs of this civilization also influenced the ancient Egyptian, Abrahamic, and Greek mythologies and traditions. And while the religion was almost suppressed by 500 C.E., devotees who became Assyrian Christians carried on some of their old habits. Because of this, the Assyrian beliefs can still influence the modern world, particularly some neo-pagan religions born in the early 20th century.

This book will help you explore the fundamental beliefs in Assyrian mythology, including those associated with sorcery and guardians. You'll also gain a comprehensive insight into the tales associated with the deities, demigods, and mighty heroes. By showing you a glimpse of their traits and associations, the relevant chapters will be a stepping stone for getting in touch with these beings. You'll receive beginner-friendly instructions on getting in touch with any beings associated with Assyrian mythology. You'll also receive instructions on how to identify the signs of them reaching out to you.

Lastly, you'll read about private and public practices used by Assyrian devotees who wish to honor a particular being or simply incorporate the Assyrian ways into their lives. The last chapter offers several easy-to-do exercises you can incorporate into your life along with hands-on instructions for preparing and performing them. This will be the conclusion of a unique journey in which you learn to understand and embrace Assyrian beliefs and practices. If you're ready to step on this path and begin your journey, keep reading.

Chapter 1:

Basics of Assyrian Mythology

Assyria was an empire in northern Mesopotamia, mainly in Turkey and Iraq. For centuries, it was a part of Babylonia, then the Mitanni kingdom, until the 14th century when it gained independence. During this time, it was one of the region's biggest and most powerful empires, influencing many cultures like Armenia and Syria. Like ancient Romans and Greeks, the Assyrians had a rich mythology reflecting their culture and beliefs.

Although Assyria influenced many Arab countries like Syria, which got its name from the Mesopotamian Empire, it didn't have an Arabic identity. Their language and culture are more ancient than that of the Arabs.

The Beliefs of Assyria Mythology

The ancient Assyrians were polytheists; they believed in the existence of multiple deities. However, some regions were henotheistic, believing in only one god but accepting that other deities also existed. There were about 2400 deities in Assyrian mythology, but some cities were dedicated to one god because they felt a rare connection with them. They built temples for their favorite deity as a home for them in the physical world when they descended from the heavens to Earth. Each god and goddess was associated with an aspect of nature, like storms, the moon, or the sun.

Although most of their gods had human bodies, some were represented by abstract symbols, natural phenomena, or animals. For instance, their supreme deity Ashur was either depicted as a bearded man inside a sun disk with wings or simply as the sun disk without human representation. Ashur, the most prominent deity in Assyrian mythology, was the king of all gods and represented righteousness and justice.

Before Ashur became the supreme god, he was a local deity worshiped in a city that was named after him. He later rose to power and has since been the most significant figure in the Assyrian empire and pantheon, and the city of Ashur became the kingdom's capital. There was a strong connection between Ashur and the Assyrian kings. According to their religious beliefs, the king was more than just a ruler; he also acted as a religious figure. Just like the gods, the public had to serve and obey their king as well. He had a sacred role as the mediator between the deities and the people. The gods expected the king to be powerful and work on appeasing them by expanding the empire, gaining wealth, and conquering other countries. Assyrian kings weren't expected to be good; they were only meant to be powerful. Even if they had to resort to violence, the gods would still be pleased with them as they wanted the kings to be feared rather than loved.

The Assyrian religion was connected with the practices and beliefs of ancient Egypt. The sacred role of the king and his association with the gods was an aspect they borrowed from the ancient Egyptians. Other similarities they shared included the worship of multiple deities and the belief in the afterlife.

The Assyrians believed in the existence of mystical and supernatural creatures and demons. Similar to all religions, demons were vicious creatures who could bring all sorts of harm and diseases to mankind. The people of Assyria suffered at their hands, so they turned to the gods for help. Scholars discovered this information through the many ancient incantations that have managed to survive. These spells reflected the suffering of the Assyrians against demons and the extent they would go to protect themselves and their loved ones. Assyrian priests created incantations by choosing specific sentences or words that had the power to ward off demons. If they didn't work, it meant that something was wrong with the words they chose. As a result, the priests saved all the phrases that succeeded in warding off demons so they could use them in various spells.

They placed statues of genii who acted as guardian angels in Assyrian mythology on each city's gate to protect against demons and other evil forces. Genii were depicted as winged creatures with beards. They held pine cones filled with water that they used to offer blessings and protect the city from danger.

Like many ancient cultures, the Assyrians were animistic. It's the belief that everything on earth, including animate and or inanimate objects, has a spiritual essence. They also believed in the existence of ghosts that belonged to the underworld. They were considered night demons who could hugely influence mankind. The only way to get rid of them is through incantations.

Temples and Shrines

The people were highly devoted to their deities and lived according to their teachings. They honored them by building ziggurats, pyramids-shaped temples that were similar to those of the ancient Egyptians. Priests ran these temples, and the people would go there to worship and appease their deities. The ziggurats were very expensive, but expenses weren't an issue when it came to honoring their gods. They were built on a large scale and decorated with luxurious adornments. There hung various artworks that illustrated various legends of the deities.

After they finished building, priests would bring the image or statue of the deity to place in their new home. Worshipers would hold festivals to celebrate this special occasion. The priests tended to these statues and took care of the temples since they represented the gods and their homes on Earth and must be protected and respected. Although there were many temples in the kingdom, the main ones were located in Kalhu, Nineveh, and Ashur. All ceremonies and rituals like divinations, exorcisms, festivals, and ceremonies took place in temples.

The people worshiped their gods by performing rituals and praying for help or guidance. They also built shrines to honor and pray for their deities, and they became a part of their day-to-day lives as well. Worshipers placed shrines in the cities, countryside, fields, or intersections and dedicated them to a specific deity. Although they weren't as big or luxurious as temples, they were no less significant. People could still use them to present offerings, express their devotions, praise the gods and goddesses, and seek their guidance in every aspect of their lives.

Priests and priestesses used temples and shrines to teach and educate people about religion, rituals, ceremonies, divinations, deities, and how to behave before the gods and goddesses.

They also built large statues of the deities and placed them in various places around the city, like shrines, temples, city gates, and public squares. The Assyrians believed that the gods and goddesses dwelled near their statues, so they decorated them with gemstones and gold.

The Assyrians also prayed and sang hymns to praise and glorify their gods and goddesses. Some of their hymns are associated with incantations and magic to force out evil spirits and demons.

The Afterlife

The Assyrians believed in life after death. Unlike the ancient Egyptians, their beliefs were simpler yet depressing. It wasn't an interesting afterlife like other ancient cultures. Although spirits would continue to exist, what they experienced was barely living. The dead spent eternity in a place called the "land of no return," which doesn't sound like a happy place. It consisted of dark rooms covered with dust with bats dressed in garments made of feathers.

They buried their dead with some of the essentials as a precaution. The kings and the rich were buried in luxurious tombs with magnificent vessels with some items like water, food, weapons, and possessions. In ancient Mesopotamia funerals, the priests would place the deceased hand on a dish of food so they would eat on their journey to the afterlife.

The rich Assyrians buried their dead at home in a room designed specifically for burial. While the poor simply dug holes in their homes to place their dead. Both lit oil lamps near burial sites as a reminder of where the dead were and that they were taken care of and protected.

When the spirits reached the land of the dead, they stood before the judges, who were called the Annunaki. Unfortunately, much of the information about the judgment has been lost throughout history. However, the Assyrians believed that the dead could come back to life. This was clear from one of the legends where the god of fertility, Tammuz, drank sacred water to return to the physical world.

Omens and Signs

Omens and signs played a big role in the Assyrian religion. The people believed that the gods communicated with them by sending messages to reveal their wishes and demands. Before making any decisions, worshipers consulted their priests to ensure the gods consented to their actions. The king had a trusted group of astrologers who would look at the movement of the stars to aid the king with major decisions concerning the state. Diviners were also able to understand omens by performing certain rituals to communicate with deities.

Omens were either good or bad and mainly relied on human actions and included "if, then" scenarios. If an individual did something, their actions would impact other people. For instance, if the king ate fish on a specific day, the whole kingdom would suffer from famine.

The Types Gods of Assyria

The Assyrian and Babylonian gods shared many similarities with one another, with one exception, Asshur, who replaced the Babylonian Marduk as the chief deity in Assyrian mythology. The pantheon of gods in Assyria was highly organized. Each God had their rank and domain. The Assyrians were warriors who were evident in the traits they associated with their gods.

In Assyrian mythology, the people perceived their deities in three ways:

Cultic Perception

Worshipers associated the deities with the temples they built for them. They believed that the gods or goddesses would manifest in the same image or statue displayed in the temple.

Natural Perception

The Assyrians associated their deities with aspects of nature like air, water, or the sun.

Metaphysical Perception

They regarded their deities as supernatural beings that didn't belong to any specific place.

Similar to other ancient cultures, there are many types of Assyrian deities.

Ashur

Ashur was the supreme god in Assyrian mythology. He was responsible for granting and removing kingship, and the king acted as his representative on Earth. He also supported the Assyrian soldiers.

Lamassu

Lamassu was a guardian god in Assyrian mythology. The purpose of this deity was to protect against evil people. His statues were placed at royal palace gates to guard the king and his family.

Enki

Enki was the god of magic, trickery, water, and creation. He was known for this intelligence and bestowed his wisdom on the people. Although his actions could seem confusing at first, his intentions were always pure. He only wanted to help others. In many legends, he was given a choice between serving humanity and obeying the other deities and always sided with mankind. He would choose to forgive and show compassion rather than be a wrathful deity.

Enlil

Enlil, the king of the deities, was the god of storms and the sky and one of the most powerful deities in Assyrian mythology. He was responsible for the fate of mankind and was both merciful and cruel. He was regarded as a father deity who watched over and cared for mankind. In fact, human beings couldn't survive without him.

Tiamat

Tiamat was the goddess of salt sea and chaos. She could be both a mother goddess and a vengeful figure. All the gods were created from her waters.

Ishtar

Ishtar was the goddess of love, sex, and war and the queen of the heavens. Although she wasn't considered a mother goddess, she was responsible for all life on Earth. Since she was associated with physical love, she became the protector of prostitutes.

Sin

Sin was the god of the moon. He had the ability to light the darkness, which made him an expert in divination. Sin played a huge role in announcing omens, determining mankind's fates, and issuing verdicts.

The Assyrians were one of the world's most powerful and influential cultures. The people were highly devoted to their deities and integrated religion into every aspect of their lives. Their gods didn't only have human physical attributes but also human characteristics. They would get angry, jealous, happy, vengeful, and even fall in love. In the next chapters, you will learn in detail about the gods and goddesses of Assyrian mythology.

Chapter 2:

Gods

In this chapter, you'll learn about the four main Assyrian deities: Ashur, Anu, Enlil, and Enki. You'll understand what their names mean, the aspects of the world they rule, and their responsibilities. This chapter offers insight into stories and mythologies that describe their behaviors and nature. You'll find out how and where they were worshipped, come across tips on how to connect with them, and signs they're reaching out to you.

Ashur

Ashur or Assur was the national deity of a capital city with the same name, where the name "Assyria" came from. He was thought to be a mere local god whose name was used while taking oaths at first. However, he later came to be known as the supreme god in the Assyrian religion when the kingdom began to expand. He was the chief god of Assur, the deity of empires and war, and was associated with the state's well-being, prosperity, and fortune. The term "Ashur" itself translates to "the good/ blesser god."

Stories and Beliefs

Based on Assyrian mythology and stories, historians believe that there are over 900 terrestrial and celestial Assyrian deities and spirits. Some of them were even adopted from Babylonian faiths. Being a supreme deity, however, Ashur wasn't related to any of these deities- he had no wife, child, attendant, or follower. The Assyrians believed that the deity would cease to exist if the empire fell.

Ashur was only worshipped in Assyria and was believed to extend his arms over the kingdom to protect it. He accompanied his high priests, who were also kings, to war. Legend says that Ashur could appoint and take away kingship.

The deity had some aspects in common with other Mesopotamian gods like Enlil and Anshar. His association with the Babylonian deity of the sky, Anshar, further supported the belief that Ashur was present during the time of creation. Some scribes even assigned Ninlil as a wife, which remains highly controversial.

How He Was Worshipped

Most Mesopotamian deities, including Ashur, had their statues taken care of by the priests in their temples. Tending to the area surrounding the statue and temple was also an act of worship. Even though there were no specific temple services or fixed prayers that the public engaged in, many people likely honored Ashur in private rituals and called the deity for guidance.

Symbols and Correspondences

The symbols associated with Ashur, which were a crown and throne, were similar to Anu's. He was mostly depicted wearing a horned helmet with arrows and a bow in his hand. The warrior deity wore feathers for a skirt and was commonly illustrated posing in a disk with wings.

Anu

The Sumerian term "Anu" translates to "heaven" or "sky." Anu is considered the personification of the celestial world or the heavens. This god, along with Enki and Enlil, makes up the triad of deities. Despite ruling over the sky and being the father of all deities, demons, and evil spirits, Anu contributed to a relatively small portion of Assyrian stories and myths. He was mostly associated with Lamashtu, the demoness who fed upon infants. He was also believed to govern the annual calendar.

Uruk, a Sumerian city that overlooked the Euphrates River, was Anu's holy city. It was a herding region, which explains his primary depiction as a great bull. Historians suggest that the deity could've initially been a member of the herders' pantheon. While some stories presented Antum as his consort, the Babylonian goddess is often confused with Ishtar.

Stories and Beliefs

Anu was labeled the highest of all gods. He was a benevolent deity who was imbued with traits from other gods and goddesses, allowing him to rise into the heavens. According to mythology, Anu wasn't associated with other deities and humans but was still regarded as the chief creator of the universe. Enlil, his son, was the only god who could interact with him and adopted his power and traits.

Anu was still popularly worshipped across Mesopotamia even when his son grew more powerful. A hymn, which was written around 2000 BCE, depicts him as a deity of high regard. It explains that other deities approached him with obedience and that he was powerful enough to travel through raging storms. The hymn reads that Anu made abundant food and drinks, was admired like a royal, and was presented with wonderful offerings, tributes, and gifts.

As time went by, fewer people prayed to the deity (at least directly); however, his power remained renowned. People still left him offerings at his temple in Uruk. Upon the fall of the Assyrian Empire, numerous deities were abandoned- those who suffered and were oppressed under the rule of Assyrian kings took out their anger on the cities, statues, and temple complexes dedicated to the deities. Anu was one of the few deities left untouched and remained venerated. His popularity was preserved until the rise of Zoroastrianism.

How He Was Worshiped

Anu was a deity of high regard and significance in several Mesopotamian cultures. He was responsible for guiding the deities and the public's religious ceremonies and was associated with agriculture and animals. While he was worshipped in several cities, he was particularly associated with Urak, his holy city. Anu and Inanna, the deity of grain, were often worshipped hand-in-hand because good weather is directly related to the abundance of crops. Anu had several temples across Mesopotamia where he was worshipped and presented with offerings.

Symbols and Correspondences

Like Ashur, the symbol of Anu is a horned crown sitting on a throne. The horns on the head ornament signify his power and strength. Anu's Sumerian equivalent, considered the primary version of the deity, was represented as a great bull. Later on, however, people started separating the deity from the figure of the bull. Stories about the respective Bull of Heaven suggested that Ashur owned it.

Enlil

The name "Enlil" translates to the "deity of Air," but the god did so much more than rule the sky. He was originally a Sumerian deity that the Assyrian borrowed from the Mesopotamian Pantheon. He was regarded as the king of all deities due to his considerable vigor and power. Enlil is a notable figure in numerous texts and is presented as the greatest god following his father, Anu.

The triad that he formed with his father and Enki ruled the underworld, Earth, and heavens. The triad also represents the sky, Earth, universe, and atmosphere. Enlil's strength and limitless force came from the fact that he was the guardian of the Tablets of Destiny. These clay tablets were thought to carry the fates of all humans and deities. No one could question or doubt the decisions that Enlil made.

Stories and Beliefs

Anzu, a Babylonian myth, depicts Enlil as the supreme ruler and the guardian of the Tablets of Destiny. The myth explains that these tablets were vital to Enlil's ability to rule over the Earth and heaven. In the story, Anzu, or the Zu bird, decides to go to war against Enlil and take the tablets so he can rule instead. As he waited for the perfect opportunity to strike, Zu noticed that Enlil had set his crown down and went to wash his face. It was the perfect opportunity for him to steal the tablets and fly away. Anu asked the deities to intervene, but no one wanted to help, which caused heaven and Earth to fall out of harmony.

Some versions of the story claim that Marduk or Ninurta were the ones who retrieved the tablets, while others suggest that it was Lugalbanda who brought them back. In all cases, however, Enlil emerged as the king and had the support of Anu. The deity was thought to be a mediating force that maintained a balance between the heavens and Earth. Enlil can wreak havoc on the world when he loses patience or becomes frustrated. One of the most famous incidents about the devastating flood was recorded in The Atrahasis epic.

How He Was Worshiped

As with all other gods, Enlil was worshiped in the multi-purpose temple complex and ziggurat. Even though they housed no special services, temples were still a crucial aspect of the community. All kinds of offerings, including incense, food, jewelry, and beverages, were given to appease and honor him. The higher priest cared for his statue and the surrounding area, as no one else could interact with the deities in their temples. Public festivals and private rituals were the only acceptable means of connection with the deities.

Symbols and Correspondences

Enlil's symbol is similar to his father's: a horned crown. He is associated with force, energy, kingship, the cardinal directions, and the planet Jupiter. The wind, double-headed axes, bulls, and eagles are also among his associations.

Enki

Enki is the deity of intelligence, fresh water, healing, and fertility. He is also associated with magic, creativity, crafts, and the art of mischief. He is usually shown as a bearded man who wears a long robe and a horned crown. The name "Enki" translates to "the ruler of the Earth."

In some illustrations, the deity is seen ascending a mountain. Others depict him standing in front of trees with streams of water running down his shoulders. The streams are believed to signify the

Tigris and Euphrates rivers and their correspondence with fresh water. The trees represent fertility and male and female figures.

Stories and Beliefs

In most mythologies, Enki tries his best to serve the best interest of his people. Unfortunately, they don't always appreciate his ways. In one story, he killed the god Apsu to protect his siblings, even though his mother's disapproved of his plan.

According to the Atrahasis, Enki saved a man by stopping Enlil from wiping out humanity. Enki also managed to bring the war to a halt by locking Nergal, the deity of warfare, in the underworld. Another story tells that he retrieved his daughter's corpse from the underworld and saved her life by doing everything in his power. He had to make poor choices to bring her back.

Even though his actions and decisions don't always make sense at first glance, the trickster deity always has a plan. That said, his mischievous nature often leads to sin. According to legend, the deity terribly missed his wife and ended up seducing his daughters, who resembled her.

How He Was Worshiped

Enki's temples comprised distribution and counseling centers, houses of healing, temples, and other holy locations. However, he was mostly worshipped in E-engur-ra, and E-abzu, which are his temples. Higher priests tended to his statue, and people interacted with him during private rituals and public celebrations.

Symbols and Correspondences

The goat, fish, elephant, turtle, and Caduceus are among his symbols. He is also associated with the image of two serpents coiling around a staff. Enki is linked to the planet Mercury and the cardinal directions, especially North.

Connecting with the Deities

To connect with any Assyrian deity, you need to take the time to learn about their mythology and the corresponding beliefs of the people. Reading in-depth about the gods gives you insight into their behaviors and interests. Meditations are commonly used in the Assyrian faith, as it helps focus one's intention. Saying prayers and calling the deity for guidance will strengthen your connection with them. Most deities accept a range of offerings and aren't particular about the gifts they receive. Make your intentions clear and regularly appease the deity.

If possible, you can visit a temple to pay your respects to the god and pray to them. Partake in public festivals to celebrate significant occasions; if you'd like to build a shrine in honor of a particular deity, clean and maintain it regularly. Decorate it with the relevant symbols, use it frequently, and consult an experienced practitioner or priest to guide you throughout the process.

There are several signs that an Assyrian deity is trying to get in touch with you. If you feel watched over or can see signs in the sky, a god might try to connect with you. Pay attention to your dreams and spiritual messages.

If you're suddenly interested in Assyrian culture and faith, then this might be a sign that an Assyrian god is trying to connect with you. Being drawn to deity-specific symbols, such as winged disks, horned crowns, or certain animals or planets, are also common indicators.

The Assyrians believed in numerous deities, and other Mesopotamian cultures, including Babylon, Akkadia, and Sumeria, heavily influenced their pantheon. However, they believed in four main gods who represented several aspects of the world, including the sky, wind, heavens, earth, sea, and fertility. Each of these deities took on unique roles and responsibilities and aimed to guide and protect their people.

Chapter 3:

Goddesses

This chapter explores the different aspects of the three most popular Assyrian goddesses: Inanna, Ninhursah, and Ereshkigal. You'll learn about their names, nature, and duties. You'll also find out about their iconography, symbols, and mythologies. In this chapter, you'll understand how they were worshiped and how you can connect with them.

Inanna

Many believe that Inanna is Sumerian for "the lady of the heavens," while others interpret it as "date clusters" rather than "heavens." You might also know the deity as Ishtar, which is a name that initially belonged to another goddess. The deity has varying family members in each tradition. She is thought to be the daughter of Ningal and Anu, Enki, or Sin, and might be the sister of Ereškigal and Utu. Inanna doesn't have a husband, but Dumuzi was believed to be her consort.

Inanna is considered the most complex and dynamic deity of her pantheon, as her traits and tales are often contradictory. Even though she is widely known as an influential, ambitious, and empowering goddess, some of her stories depict her as a coy maiden whose potential and the patriarchy restricts freedom. She is unknowingly pushed into an arranged marriage to Dumuzi and is keen to maintain her boundaries with him even when they're together without supervision. This goes against her temptress aura in the Epic of Gilgameš, where she tries to take the protagonist as her lover. To her surprise, however, he rejected her because of her extensive history with men.

The main similarity between the coy and femme fatale representations of the deity is her sexuality. Her sexual nature is evident in various Sumerian poetry pieces and the Epic of Gilgameš. Many people prayed to her when they needed help with issues like unrequited love or impotency. The goddess is also the deity and patroness of prostitutes.

Inanna loves battle as much as she enjoys intimacy and passion. She is associated with military and royal prowess due to her war-like nature. This aspect of Inanna, however, wasn't evident before the Old Akkadian period when scripts mainly focused on her femininity.

The deity's masculine and war-like aspects were not the only traits she leveraged when exercising political power. She also capitalized on her feminine nature to gain political power. Her relationship with Dumuzi was most likely an intellectual setup.

Stories and Beliefs

According to the myth Inanna and Šu-kale-tuda, a gardener boy, raped the goddess while she was sleeping soundly under a tree. Raging with anger, the deity sets out to find the boy in hiding. The route that the deity takes is similar to Venus' astral track. She also mimics Venus' cycle in the myth, Inanna and Enki, where she travels from Uruk, her hometown, to Eridu, the city of Enki, and back again. Historians suggest that Assyrians used to embark on the goddess' journey during festivals.

In another story, Inanna journeys to the underworld and back. There, she sits on Ereškigal's throne, which angers the other deities in the pantheon, who turns her into a corpse. Ninšubur, who's Inanna's sukkal or second goddess in command, asks for Enki's help, and together they bring Inanna back to the world. The inscriptions found in Ancient Assyrian graves mostly depict Inanna-related iconography because of her trips back and from the world of the dead.

How She Was Worshiped

The rituals and practices used to worship Inanna varied depending on the period and location. The deity, however, had several temples built in her honor all over Mesopotamia, with Ururk being her main city of worship. Higher priests maintained her temples and statues and conducted daily rituals. Worshippers presented her with foods like fruits, grains, meats, drinks, and other offerings like precious metals.

The deity was associated with the arts, especially dancing and singing, which were incorporated into her rituals and acts of worship. Inanna was honored at several points during the years, such as New Year's and the Atiku festival, which commemorated her victory over Kur.

Symbols and Correspondences

Inanna's various characteristics were reflected in her vas iconography. A bundle of reeds often represents her. The Warka or Uruk Vase shows the deity standing in front of two gateposts. Most depictions of the deity in her human forms show her fully nude. She is sometimes found holding her cape open to reveal herself.

To illustrate her masculine and war-like nature, Inanna was sometimes shown wearing a trimmed robe and had weapons peeking out from her shoulders. She usually held a weapon and was even illustrated with a beard.

In her warrior form, the deity is associated with lions and can sometimes be seen standing on the animal's back. An eight-pointed star is used to symbolize the astral nature of the goddess. Inanna is associated with the colors red and blue and the stones carnelian and lapis lazuli. Some people think that red and blue are symbolic of her feminine and masculine natures, respectively.

Ninhursag

Ninhursag is believed to be the most significant deity in the pantheon. She is one of the oldest goddesses, and is known for her role as the "Sumerian Mother Goddess." The goddess partook in the creation of all human and divine life. Many myths call the goddess by different names, depending on her role in the tale.

In Sumer, the goddess was associated with fertility and the act of nurture. There, she was given the name Damkina, took Sul-pa-e, a minor underworld deity, as her husband, and had 3 children together. Ninhursag, however, is most commonly known to be Enki's wife.

The name "Ninhursag" translates to the "Lady of the Mountain." This name comes from Lugale, a poem that tells the story of Ninurta, the goddess' son and the deity of warfare and hunting, who defeats a demon and his army before building a mountain of their bodies. He then attributes his victory to his mother Ninmah, which translates to "glorious queen," and renames her "Ninhursag."

Stories and Beliefs

In the myth of Atrahasis, Ninhursag created mankind by mixing clay with the intelligence and blood of a deity who sacrificed himself for the rise of humanity. Another story tells how Enki and Ninmah created humankind during a competition where they made creatures using clay. Many believe that Enki decided to create humans to relieve some of the burdens and responsibilities of the gods. All deities mourned when Enlil gave rise to the Great Flood, and Ninhursag wept the loss of her children. The goddess' significance was diminished when Enki replaced her role as the creator. This also led to her decreased relevance to feminine attributes and functions. Historians suggest that during this time, the goddesses had started to lose their influence and were becoming marginalized.

While Ninhursag's name comes last in the list of the 4 creator deities, she was likely held in higher regard during earlier periods (her name certainly came before Enki's). She remained one of the Seven Divine Powers, and even though each of the 7 deities had a unique gift to offer humanity, Ninhursag is superior to all humans and is honored among the deities. She is regarded as the guardian of all women and children and oversees birth and conception.

How She Was Worshiped

The deity was mainly worshiped in the city of Adab but was associated with several temples, such as the Girsu temple, throughout Mesopotamia. Worshippers made her offerings of drinks, food, and other objects, and even sometimes made her animal sacrifices. Worshippers who associated the deity with agriculture might have made offerings of grains and crops, while those who associated her with water likely made her offerings at wells and springs. Ninhursag was also celebrated on many occasions, such as the Ariku festival, which marked the start of the agricultural season. Rituals, prayers, and offerings are performed in honor of the goddess during festivals and celebrations.

Symbols and Correspondences

The Ω symbol is used to represent the goddess because ancient Assyrians thought it looked similar to a uterus. They often illustrated a knife beside the symbol, which is used to cut the umbilical cord. However, representations of the deity in human form are often hard to distinguish from illustrations of other goddesses.

Ninhursag is associated with mountains, snakes, cows, lionesses, and trees, as they represent many of her aspects, including strength, fertility, protection, nurturing, and growth.

Ereshkigal

The name "Ereshkigal" translates to the "Queen of the Great Place/ Below." The word "great" here reflects the size rather than the quality of the place. The underworld is not a desirable place to visit- whoever went there wouldn't be able to return. The land of the dead was thought to exist beneath the Earth under the Mountains of Sunset. The souls who ended up there ate dust and drank from mud.

Ereshkigal is the governor of the dead and responsible for keeping those who passed onto the underworld in her realm. Ereshkigal is supposed to stop humans from learning about the underworld and the afterlife and prevent them from entering this realm. Her palace, Ganzir, has 7 gates and is located near the gates of the land of the dead. Ereshkigal was the sole queen of the underworld until she took the deity Nergal, who helps her rule the underworld semiannually, as her consort.

Stories and Beliefs

The goddess is widely feared due to her duty as the keeper of the dead and the queen of the underworld. However, she is highly esteemed and respected. She's featured in the myth of the Descent of Inanna, which has been falsely interpreted for centuries. Many suggest that the tale tells about a woman's journey to discover and embrace her true self. While the poem does show Inanna coming to terms with her darker nature, this is not the plot nor the essence of the tale. Inanna is the protagonist of the myth and is presented as a heroic archetype, but this doesn't overshadow her selfish and egotistic aspect. Instead of praising Inanna, the poem concludes by celebrating Ereshkigal.

How She Was Worshiped

Ereshkigal was mostly worshiped in Assyria and Babylonia, where people left her offerings at her temple. E-anna-kurkurra, the temple dedicated to Ereshkigal and Nergal, was located in the ancient Babylonian city Kutha. Worshippers also used divination and necromancy to honor the deity. Since they believed they could communicate with the dead, they contacted Ereshkigal as an intermediary. They also used oracles and the help of mediums to gain insight into the future. The deity was usually invoked during burial and funerary practices and rituals. People mainly prayed to the goddess and appeased her to ensure a safe journey to the underworld after their deaths.

Symbols and Correspondences

The iconography and symbols of the goddess are unknown. The only possible representation of Ereshkigal comes from what we know as the Burney Relief. This relief is a terra-cotta plaque that carries an illustration of a winged naked woman. The woman carries symbols of powers with her wings pointing downward. Her feet are shaped like talons, and she stands on two lions that lie on tiny illustrations of mountains. There are two owls standing on either side.

The relief is generally thought to portray Ereshkigal. However, some people suggest that it depicts either the demon Lilith or the goddess Inanna. Several other plaques also portray the same woman despite the Burney Relief being the most popular one.

According to Mesopotamian beliefs, one would only illustrate a figure or create a structure of something if one wanted to bring attention to it. For instance, worshippers created statues of their deities to honor them- they thought they served as homes to the gods and goddesses. Since people feared Ereshkigal, they didn't want to bring much attention to her, which is why her iconography is still undeciphered.

Connecting with the Deities

You need to take the time to learn about the goddesses to connect with them effectively. Determine how you relate to them and the aspects of your life that they can guide you in. Incorporate meditation practices into your routine to open your consciousness and improve your ability to deliver and receive messages from the spiritual realm.

You can explore divination practices if you'd like, as they were integral to ancient Assyrian culture. Learn about different tools and consult with a diviner who can help you reach out to the goddess you'd like to work with.

Chapter 4:

Demigods and Heroes

This chapter explores the world of the demigods and heroes of Assyrian mythology. You'll learn about the differences between demigods and heroes and their roles in Assyrian mythology. Besides their name, you'll learn about their behavior, methods of worship, association, and how to call on them.

The terms hero and demigod are often used interchangeably, even though their meaning can differ. While some demigods can be heroes, not all heroes are demigods. A demigod is the offspring of a mortal and a deity. They often possess inhuman strengths and characteristics but are rarely immortal. Several Assyrian demigods are known for their heroic deeds and contribution to people's lives. They can be excellent guides or protectors even in modern times. Heroes, on the other hand, are mortal. They aren't stronger than any other person. However, they are often smarter, faster, and wiser.

Through courageous and noble acts, heroes rise to fame and are forever remembered as someone people could turn to in need. According to Assyrian mythology, the souls of the heroes live on in the spiritual world, and they, too, can assist in challenging contemporary situations.

Adapa

Adapa is a prominent figure in the Assyrian religion. There isn't any clear evidence of where this mythical being got its name. However, the term "Adapa" in the ancient language of the region is often mentioned as an epithet translated as "wise." This association reveals that Adapa was known for his wisdom and ability to rule justly. Besides becoming the archetype of a wise ruler, Adapa is also known for refusing the gift of immortality - albeit this wasn't a conscious decision on his part.

According to most lore, Adapa was a mortal man serving as a priest in the temple of Ea. Other myths suggest that Ea was Adapa's father, making him a demigod. However, all versions agree that while Adapa had the wisdom of the gods, he wasn't immortal. One of the most prominent tales is about Adapa's death and return to Earth. One day, when he was fishing at a river, his boat was overturned by strong winds. Adapa, furious with the wind, broke its wings. Noticing that the wind wasn't blowing for several days, the gods called Adapa to ask him about his actions. When entering the gates of heaven to meet with the gods, Adapa was warned not to eat or drink anything in this realm as these could kill him. He took the garments and oils offered to them by the gods but said that he felt very sad that the gods wouldn't pay as much attention to the Earth as they should. He refused the water and food he was offered - which were revealed to be the water and food of life that could've given him immortality. After this, he was punished for breaking the wings of the wind and for refusing the gift of immortality and was returned to Earth. His punishment reflected in diseases that appeared between people.

Some consider the epithet of Adapa an equivalent to Apkallu, the term that denotes seven different demigods. These are also said to be wise beings, often described as part man, part fish. They're credited for giving people life, intelligence, God's fate, a roof over their heads, fertile pastures, cities, and the ability for their souls to rise to heaven.

In ancient times, Adapa's name was often used to invoke his power in exorcism rituals or when rulers had to be legitimized. You can still call on him to empower you with wisdom or confidence in your knowledge in a particular field. To evoke him, you need to say: I am Adapa. You can also connect with him through symbols of wisdom and justice, including books, scales, prayers, and other symbols of faith. If you notice that you suddenly have a clarification of an idea, this is a sign that Adapa is helping you.

Enkidu

A legendary figure in Assyrian mythology, Enkidu is closely associated with Gilgamesh. Enkidu, whose name is translated as "the good man," was characterized by a unique appearance. Often depicted as the "wild man" or the "bull man," Enkidu always accompanied Gilgamesh on his ventures. According to one tale, the two ventured into the Forest of the Cedars and headed towards the seven mountains. Enkidu warned his comrade about the magical creature Huwawa, which inhabited the region, as they were about to traverse the hills. Enkidu knew that this being had seven supernatural powers, so he helped his friend set up a trap for it. After curing the trees at the base of the mountain, Huwawa appeared, and the two offered him seven gifts in exchange for not using his seven powers. Huwawa accepted the deal, but Enkidu and Gilgamesh attacked and killed it. The two were reproached by the gods for their actions, and the seven power were distributed into the forest, reed beds, rivers, fields, palaces, lions, and the goddess Nungal. To this day, the fascination laced with fear of all these places, items, and beings is explained by the gifts they were given due to Enkidu's actions.

Another myth recounts how Enkidu saved Gilgamesh from an enraged bull, who was sent after him because he infuriated a goddess. After grabbing the bull's tail and holding it steady with his supernatural strength, Enkidu helped his friend kill the animal. They distributed their meat among the people and made its horns into an ornament used for holding oil in rituals. The latter has become a symbol universally associated with Enkidu - often used in public and private rites devoted to him. You can honor and call on Enkidu through symbols like bulls, lions, oak trees, harvest from a field or river, or items of value. He can help you gain strength to overcome challenging times, and you'll definitely feel his presence through the sense of empowerment and redoubled confidence just when you need these the most.

Lugalbanda

Lugalbanda was a mortal king who became deified due to his heroic deeds in various Mesopotamian regions. His name can be translated as "the fierce king," indicating his power and strength - both of which he was known for from an early age.

There are several stories attesting to the deeds of Lugalbanda. One of the most prominent ones is the story of Lugalbanda and the Anzu bird. Depicted as a lion-headed eagle, the Anzu birds lived in the mountains, where Lugalbanda came across a chick during his travels as a young soldier. After feeding the chick, the parent birds became so grateful to Lugalbanda that they gifted him the power of speed. After joining his king - who was trying to conduct a siege of their enemy's land- Luganbanda volunteered to travel over seven mountains to seek the help of the goddess Inanna. He was successful, and after carrying back the goddess's advice, he helped his king defeat the enemy.

In various Assyrian lore, Lugalbanda is associated with the mighty king Shulgi, who was believed to be his son. He is also linked to Gilgamesh, who has a different connection to Lugalbanda, depending on the storyline. Some tales refer to Gilgamesh as the son of Lugalbanda. Whereas others claim that Gilgamesh only venerated Lugalbanda as his god.

After being deified, Lugalbanda was worshiped in temples elevated in his honor and the honor of his equally powerful daughter, who became the first priestess of Lugalbanda. As he was first and foremost known as a warrior, this is a cue on how to honor him. You can use symbols of strength, ancient weapons, birds, and speed. Seeing a bird flying fast or noticing the time fly by when you're traveling is said to be a sign of Lugalbandas's presence.

Shamhat

According to Assyrian lore, Shamhat was created by the deities to bring Enkidu into civilization.

Translated as "the luscious one," the name of Shamhat is associated with feminine powers, sensuality, and sexuality - and for a good reason. Her role was to seduce Enkidu, who until then lived among wild animals, having considered an animal himself due to his appearance. However, because she was able to convert him from a wild bull-man into a civilized warrior, she is accredited for her powerful deed as Enkidu becomes the friend, comrade, and savior of Gilgamesh. However, Enkidu himself blamed her for the experiences that led to his death after being civilized. According to the lore, while on his deathbed, Enkidu cursed Shamhat, causing her to become an outcast. While she humbly accepts her destiny, the deities remind Enkidu that Shamhat gave him a home, clothes, and food. She treated him in a civilized manner when he still was a wild man and accepted him for who he was, just as she accepted him as a warrior. Realizing his mistake, Enkidu overturns his curse and blesses Shamhat with the beauty that makes all men desire her.

Shamhat is revered as a mother or companion figure to Enkidu and later to people. In rituals dedicated to her, she is offered wine, jewelry, food, and fine clothes. She can be a great force to call on when you need to raise your self-confidence regarding your appearance. You can also honor her by wearing your best clothes and jewelry and saying a prayer to her at a shrine dedicated to her.

Sammu-rammat

Known in popular culture as Semiramis, Sammu-rammat was a mortal princess who became the wife of an Assyrian king. According to some sources, her name is translated as "mother right" due to her association with fertility and motherhood. Later on, she came to a position where she ruled over the destiny of many great people and ultimately became a demigod. According to another story, Semiramis was the daughter of a mortal man and the fish and bird goddess named Derceto. Because of this, Semiramis is said to have the power to transform into a bird.

The name Semiramis is associated with social and religious innovations, including erecting temples and shrines for female deities or popularizing the use of harvest materials in rituals when venerating said goddesses. According to certain myths, Semiramis also took part in the creation of lakes, fields, and people. The goddess was also claimed as a mother by several overlords who wanted to assume the throne of Assyria - which also explains how she became the archetype of the mother figure.

Semiramis can be called on through rituals involving the harvest and other agricultural practices. These customs stem from the fact that public rituals had more of a political role after her rule. So, those who wanted to honor deities or demigods through more traditional customs could only do so in mountain tops, fields, or at home. You can connect with her in either of these places and ask for her assistance with fertility, protection, or guidance in aspects associated with children, motherhood, home, and family.

She is also linked to prosperity, as during her rule, Assyria became one of the region's most economically and culturally thriving countries. Besides erecting religious and communal buildings, she is praised for cutting roads through mountains and facilitating travel through these regions. Her influences were felt in other cultures, too, even the much older Babylonian beliefs.

Because her actions extended to various aspects of life, Semiramis has never become associated with local forces - unlike many other female heroes or demigods in other belief systems. She was able to create a link between the natural world and the civilized one. Even today, she can help those seeking a connection between the ancient Assyrian culture and themselves as recipients of this wisdom. Whether you view her as a queen, a high priestess, or a demigod, you can identify with her on many levels.

Other sources claim that her name is translated as "the one guarded by a dove," indicating the importance of this magnificent bird to the life of Semiramis. This belief stems from a story surrounding the birth of Semiramis. According to this, Semiramis was abandoned by her mother soon after her birth. Fortunately, she was protected by a dove until a man found her and took her in to raise her. The dove is still considered sacred in many Mesopotamian territories, including Assyria. Because doves guarded Semiramis as a child, she is also associated with this bird. In ancient times, every home had a household dove to represent the protective power of Semiramis over the home. You can also use white doves to call on her.

Chapter 5:

Practices

The Assyrians honored their gods through many practices and traditions like exorcism, divination, and sacrifices. There are various traditions in every aspect of Assyrian mythology, like burials, marriage, birth, and many others. The priests and priestesses in the Assyrian religion are highly respected among worshipers, and they play major roles in performing rituals and ceremonies. The purpose of these practices isn't only to appease the gods but also to assist the people and guarantee the community's well-being. Some of these practices are performed publicly, like in the streets or temples, while others are performed at home using shrines.

Although some of the modern-day Assyrian practices have ancient roots, their origins aren't clear. Holding on to these traditions showed their respect for older generations and the values and wisdom of the Assyrian religion and culture.

As a result, many of these rituals were integrated into their daily lives and became significant to their existence.

Main practices in Assyrian Mythology

Public Devotion

One of the things that unite Assyrians all over the world is their religious customs and traditions. Although some of these practices have changed over the years, they still carry the Assyrian essence, culture, and main beliefs. Many public rituals performed at weddings or after the birth of a child are meant to unite people and remind them of what they share in common instead of their differences.

Divination

Divination is one of the most significant practices in the Assyrian religion. They believe the gods can communicate with them through divination. By interpreting various aspects of nature, like reading the stars or watching birds fly, they can figure out the will of the gods and goddesses. Priests and priestesses are experts in divination, and the people usually go to temples to seek their wisdom, ask about the future, or for insight into the deities' will.

The main purpose of divination is to seek and find divine manifestation through the many messages hidden in nature. These messages aren't obvious or self-explanatory. For instance, predicting future events requires strong interpretation skills since they aren't self-evident.

In ancient Assyrian mythology, diviners practiced different types of divination that are split into two: spontaneity and directness.

Spontaneous Divination

- pontaneous or natural phenomena that mankind has no influence or control over, like volcanoes or earthquakes.
- Seeking a specific message in a dream where the person looks for it instead of the deity directly showing it to them.

Direct Divination

- These messages, as the name suggests, are more direct. For instance, you can get the message orally from a prophecy.

- Dreams where the deities can send messages directly to the person in their sleep.
- Indirect messages through natural phenomena like a solar or lunar eclipse.

The storm god Adad and the sun god Shamash are associated with divination. Worshipers in ancient Assyria would pray to them to deliver their messages either directly or spontaneously.

Exorcisms

The Assyrians are afraid and wary of spiritual or demonic possessions and usually take every precaution against them. When someone is possessed, the priests and priestesses perform an exorcism to drive out the demons and cure them of the evil that has touched them. They usually perform ceremonies or rituals or recite incantations.

Besides priests, an exorcist or ašipu performs the ritual. They are highly trained individuals who cure people of supernatural afflictions using incantations and rituals. However, they aren't the ones that come up with the incantations; they are bestowed on them by the gods.

Childbirth

The Assyrians perform certain customs and rituals when a child is born. Women give birth at home with the help of a midwife or a neighbor on the floor, not on a bed.

Instructions:

- After the baby is born, the midwife wipes them with salt.
- She then pulls the child's legs up and places their arms by their sides, then wraps them tightly in swaddling clothes. This tradition is meant to prevent the child from moving while they are sleeping.
- She then folds a piece of cotton cloth into a triangle and wraps it tightly around their head.
- Afterward, she straps the baby with cloth bands attached to the cradle's frame.
- The child should be placed on his back under a mosquito net and left there for hours, unable to move.
- Babies don't wear diapers; instead, the midwife places a jar in a hole through the crib

for the newborn's bowel movements. She also puts a wooden waxed tube between the child's legs to transfer the urine to the jar.

Before the mother's milk flows, close family members usually nurse the newborn. The mother should be secluded and refrain from bathing for forty days from the day she gives birth if the baby is a boy, but if it is a girl, she should be secluded for sixty days. Her relatives and neighbors usually take care of her by bringing food and looking after the baby when she's busy. The mother usually places an iron tool under her pillow to protect herself and the baby against harm and evil spirits. She should keep the tool with her wherever she goes inside the house to keep the demon Lilith away from her and the child. Burning incense in the baby's room is necessary as a protection against evil. They should never be named after a relative who died in childhood.

Marriage

Marriage is held in high regard among the Assyrians. It doesn't only represent the union of two people but of two families. Even though couples can get divorced, it is frowned upon and unaccepted in this religion. Arranged marriages are very common among Assyrians, and it is usually the father who makes the choice.

Before and during the wedding, certain rituals must take place.

Henna

Henna is a substance similar to a tattoo, but it isn't permanent. The day before the wedding, all the bride's female friends and family members throw a party at her house. The bride and groom should place their pinkies in the henna and wrap their fingers together with a ribbon. It is a fun ceremony where guests dance and have fun.

Washing the Groom

Before the wedding, the groom's male friends, neighbors, and family members go to his house to cut his hair and shave his face. He should then bathe from head to toe to remove any evil forces.

Burakha

A priest usually performs this ritual where he spends an hour blessing the bride and groom. He then pinches the groom with a needle to ward off evil spirits.

During the wedding, the groom's close family members stand outside as guards to protect them against supernatural forces or the evil eye, while the bride's female relatives should stand directly behind her for protection as well.

Private Devotions

Worshipers can worship their gods or practice rituals in the privacy of their homes. One of the most popular practices is to build an altar to honor your favorite deity. You can pray at it and present offerings to appease the deity.

Instructions:

- Before you build the altar, set an intention that you are building it to worship a specific deity (mention them by name).
- Next, choose a place to set your altar. It can be a shelf or a spare moon; it's your choice. However, it should be a private, quiet space with no distractions. Keep it away from people who can knock it over or disturb it.

- Choose the objects you will add to your altar, like a statue, images, or symbols of the deity. Choose as many as you like, and you can even include offerings.
- Clean the altar and place the objects in an organized manner.
- Worship at your altar every day.
- Keep it maintained and clean, and never ignore it to avoid angering the deity.

Many of the ancient Assyrian rituals are still practiced to this day, like the marriage and birth rituals. This reflects the people's devotion to their religion as they still hold on to their ancient beliefs. Some of these rituals remain unchanged. Worshipers are strict in abiding by them and refuse to alter or modernize them. Holding on to these rituals and traditions isn't just about religion; it is also about protecting their roots and preserving their culture. If modern Assyrians stay loyal to their ancient practices, this culture will be able to survive till the end of time. It has been around for thousands of years, thanks to the devotion of its followers.

Conclusion

It's safe to say that throughout this epic journey of Assyrian mythology, you were presented with the most prominent figures and principles in this belief system. You've learned about the role of the land on which devotees live, Assyrian thoughts about life after death, and the many deities they worship as guardians and providers. While much of the beliefs were borrowed from the much older religion of ancient Babylonia, the Assyrian devotees' customs and practices also impacted other religions in Mesopotamia, Greece, and other ancient territories. The main reason behind this influence lies in the polytheistic nature of the Assyrian belief system and the hierarchy between the gods.

You were introduced to powerful gods and goddesses like Enlil, An, Enki, Inanna, Ninhursag, Ereshkigal, and other prominent figures in the Assyrian pantheon. You've learned about their role in people's lives, tales supporting their background and powers, how to connect with them, and how they might communicate with you. Similarly, you've had the chance to explore the lore of the mighty heroes and beautiful queens - some of whom were demigods - while others were mere mortals who will forever be remembered for their courageous acts, nobility, and benevolent nature.

As you've read about how the Assyrians worshiped their deities and heroes, you might have been inspired to connect to one of them yourself. If this was the case, you were happy to discover that the last chapter provided even more ways to practice the Assyrian religion. In ancient times, public devotions were more popular and involved large gatherings at temples and shrines where devotees took time to honor and cherish a particular deity at a time. More and more devotees pay homage to a personal god, goddess, demigod, or hero who acts as their guide, healer, or protector in times of need. Practices like prayers, divination, and spiritual purification are common in the Assyrian religion, and you can easily incorporate them into your day-to-day life if you wish to embrace them.

References

7 ancient Assyrian wedding traditions you might not know about. (2018, April 19). Wedded Wonderland. https://weddedwonderland.com/7-ancient-assyrian-wedding-traditions-you-might-not-know-about/

Adapa. (n.d.). Wikiwand. https://wikiwand.com/en/Adapa

An/Anu (god). (n.d.). http://oracc.museum.upenn.edu/amgg/listofdeities/an/

Assyria, religion, and middlebury's relief. (2020, April 26). Esri. https://storymaps.arcgis.com/stories/f9b5df5f9502418c9e61b9ffc3d694fb

Assyria: Civilization and empire. (2016, October 20). TimeMaps. https://timemaps.com/civilizations/assyria/

Assyrian & Babylonian Gods and Goddesses. (n.d.). Study.Com. https://study.com/academy/lesson/assyrian-babylonian-gods-and-goddesses.html

Assyrian & Babylonian Gods and Goddesses. (n.d.). Study.Com. https://study.com/academy/lesson/assyrian-babylonian-gods-and-goddesses.html

Assyrian Mythology. (n.d.). Upenn.edu. https://digital.library.upenn.edu/women/eagle/congress/reedea.html

Assyrian Mythology. (n.d.). Upenn.Edu. https://digital.library.upenn.edu/women/eagle/congress/reedea.html

Assyrian rituals of life-cycle events. (n.d.-a). Aina.org. http://www.aina.org/articles/yoab.htm

Assyrian rituals of life-cycle events. (n.d.-b). Aina.org. http://www.aina.org/articles/yoab.htm

Assyrian wedding rituals. (n.d.). Ankawa.com. http://english.ankawa.com/?p=5796

Babylonia and Assyria, Religion of in the international standard Bible encyclopedia. (n.d.). International Standard Bible Encyclopedia Online. https://

www.internationalstandardbible.com/B/babylonia-and-assyria-religion-of.html

Busy Hopper. (n.d.). Anu-father of the gods. As.ua.edu. https://ancientart.as.ua.edu/anu-father-of-the-gods/

Editors, C. R. (2014). The Assyrians: The history of the most prominent empire of the ancient near east. Createspace Independent Publishing Platform.

Enlil/Ellil (god). (n.d.). http://oracc.museum.upenn.edu/amgg/listofdeities/enlil/index.html

Ereškigal (goddess). (n.d.).http://oracc.museum.upenn.edu/amgg/listofdeities/erekigal/index.html

Gabbay, U. (n.d.). The practice of divination in the ancient near east. Thetorah.com. https://www.thetorah.com/article/the-practice-of-divination-in-the-ancient-near-east

Gabbay, U. (n.d.). The practice of divination in the ancient near east. Thetorah.com. https://www.thetorah.com/article/the-practice-of-divination-in-the-ancient-near-east

Helena. (2021, January 24). How to build an altar at home for spiritual self-care. Disorient. https://disorient.co/build-an-altar/

Hero vs. Demigod - What's the difference? (2014, July 16). WikiDiff. https://wikidiff.com/hero/demigod

Human-headed winged bull. (n.d.). Uchicago.edu. https://www.lib.uchicago.edu/collex/exhibits/discovery-collection-memory-oriental-institute-100/human-headed-winged-bull/

Inana/Ištar (goddess). (n.d.).http://oracc.museum.upenn.edu/amgg/listofdeities/inanaitar/

Ishtar. (n.d.). Brooklynmuseum.org. https://www.brooklynmuseum.org/eascfa/dinner_party/place_settings/ishtar

Konstantopoulos, G. (2020). Demons and exorcism in ancient Mesopotamia. Religion Compass, 14(10), 1–14. https://doi.org/10.1111/rec3.12370

Lendering, J. (n.d.). Lamassu (bull-man). Livius.org. https://www.livius.org/articles/mythology/lamassu-bull-man/

Lugalbanda. (n.d.). Wikiwand. https://wikiwand.com/en/Lugalbanda

Mark, J. J. (2010). Inanna. World History Encyclopedia. https://www.worldhistory.org/Inanna/

Mark, J. J. (2017a). Anu. World History Encyclopedia. https://www.worldhistory.org/Anu/

Mark, J. J. (2017a). Assur. World History Encyclopedia. https://www.worldhistory.org/assur/

Mark, J. J. (2017a). Ereshkigal. World History Encyclopedia. https://www.worldhistory.org/Ereshkigal/

Mark, J. J. (2017b). Assur. World History Encyclopedia. https://www.worldhistory.org/assur/

Mark, J. J. (2017b). Enki. World History Encyclopedia. https://www.worldhistory.org/Enki/

Mark, J. J. (2017b). Ninhursag. World History Encyclopedia. https://www.worldhistory.org/Ninhursag/

Mark, J. J. (2017c). Enki. World History Encyclopedia. https://www.worldhistory.org/Enki/

Mark, J. J. (2017d). Enlil. World History Encyclopedia. https://www.worldhistory.org/Enlil/

Mark, J. J. (2018). Assyria. World History Encyclopedia. https://www.worldhistory.org/assyria/

Meek, T. J. (1917). Babylonian and Assyrian MythologyMyths and legends of Babylonia and Assyria. Lewis Spence. The American Journal of Theology, 21(3), 459–460. https://doi.org/10.1086/479861

Mesopotamia daily life in Assyria. (n.d.). HISTORY'S HISTORIES
You Are History. We Are the Future. http://www.historyshistories.com/mesopotamia-daily-life-in-assyria.html

Mother goddess (ninmah, nintud/r, belet-ili). (n.d.).http://oracc.museum.upenn.edu/amgg/listofdeities/mothergoddess/index.html

MYTHS OF BABYLONIA AND ASSYRIA. (n.d.). Gutenberg.Org. https://www.gutenberg.org/files/16653/16653-h/16653-h.htm#id2544669

Nair, N. (2022, October 10). Enlil : The king of gods. Mythlok. https://mythlok.com/enlil/

Nanna/Suen/Sin (god). (n.d.). http://oracc.museum.upenn.edu/amgg/listofdeities/nannasuen/

No title. (n.d.-a). Study.com. https://study.com/academy/lesson/ancient-assyria-religion-death-burial.html

No title. (n.d.-a). Study.com. https://study.com/learn/lesson/mesopotamian-god-ashur-summary-history.html

No title. (n.d.-b). Study.com. https://study.com/academy/lesson/ancient-assyria-religion-death-burial.html

No title. (n.d.-b). Study.com. https://study.com/learn/lesson/mesopotamian-god-ashur-summary-history.html

No title. (n.d.-c). Study.com. https://study.com/academy/lesson/mesopotamian-god-ashur-definition-history.html

No title. (n.d.-c). Study.com. https://study.com/learn/lesson/babylonian-assyrian-gods-deities-family-tree-mythology.html

No title. (n.d.-d). Study.com. https://study.com/academy/lesson/assyrian-babylonian-gods-and-goddesses.html

Salem, C. (2023, January 29). The majestic and complex world of the ancient Assyrian religion: Gods, rituals, and beliefs. Nineveh Rising. https://www.ninevehrising.org/post/the-majestic-and-complex-world-of-the-ancient-assyrian-religion-gods-rituals-and-beliefs

Salem, C. (2023, January 29). The majestic and complex world of the ancient Assyrian religion: Gods, rituals, and beliefs. Nineveh Rising. https://www.ninevehrising.org/post/the-majestic-and-complex-world-of-the-ancient-assyrian-religion-gods-rituals-and-beliefs

Shamhat. (n.d.). Wikiwand. https://wikiwand.com/en/Shamhat

Shamhat. (n.d.). Wikiwand. https://wikiwand.com/en/Shamhat

Sutori. (n.d.). Sutori.com. https://www.sutori.com/en/story/gods-and-goddesses-of-ancient-assyria--XnvXBQHbzXYvt24Fo6bvY1hL

The Editors of Encyclopedia Britannica. (2021). Ninurta. In Encyclopedia Britannica.

The Editors of Encyclopedia Britannica. (2022). Ishtar. In Encyclopedia Britannica.

The Editors of Encyclopedia Britannica. (2022a). Ishtar. In Encyclopedia Britannica.

The Editors of Encyclopedia Britannica. (2022b). Assyria. In Encyclopedia Britannica.

The Editors of Encyclopedia Britannica. (2023). Anu. In Encyclopedia Britannica.

The Pantheon of Assyria [chapter VII]. (2012, October 9). Wisdomlib.org. https://www.wisdomlib.org/mesopotamian/book/myths-and-legends-of-babylonia-and-assyria/d/doc7167.html

Tiamat (goddess). (n.d.). http://oracc.museum.upenn.edu/amgg/listofdeities/tiamat/index.html

Printed by Libri Plureos GmbH in Hamburg, Germany